THE UNDERGROUND RAILROAD

Nancy Allen

Educational Media

rourkeeducationalmedia.com

Before Reading:

Building Academic Vocabulary and Background Knowledge

Before reading a book, it is important to tap into what your child or students already know about the topic. This will help them develop their vocabulary, increase their reading comprehension, and make connections across the curriculum.

1. Look at the cover of the book. What will this book be about?
2. What do you already know about the topic?
3. Let's study the Table of Contents. What will you learn about in the book's chapters?
4. What would you like to learn about this topic? Do you think you might learn about it from this book? Why or why not?
5. Use a reading journal to write about your knowledge of this topic. Record what you already know about the topic and what you hope to learn about the topic.
6. Read the book.
7. In your reading journal, record what you learned about the topic and your response to the book.
8. After reading the book complete the activities below.

Content Area Vocabulary
Read the list. What do these words mean?

abolitionists
agents
Canada
conductors
Confederacy
Emancipation Proclamation
free states
fugitive
masters
passengers
plantation
seceded
Seminoles
slave states
slaves
stations
Thirteenth Amendment
Underground Railroad

After Reading:

Comprehension and Extension Activity

After reading the book, work on the following questions with your child or students in order to check their level of reading comprehension and content mastery.

1. How did the Fugitive Slave Law affect the runaway slaves trying to go North? (Summarize)
2. Why was slavery one of the reasons for the Civil War? (Asking questions)
3. Why didn't slaves know the geography or direction in which they traveled? (Inferring)
4. What are the Emancipation Proclamation and Thirteenth Amendment? What is the difference between the two? (Asking questions)
5. Why do you think slaves did not work on Sundays? (Inferring)

Extension Activity

Learn more! Abolitionists were people who wanted to stop slavery. There were several mentioned in the book. Research one of the abolitionists introduced in the book or another known abolitionist. Write an informational essay on the life of the person you chose and how they impacted slavery. Share your research with a classmate, teacher, or parent.

TABLE OF CONTENTS

Chapter 1

AN UNUSUAL NAME

The **Underground Railroad** was not underground, and it was not a railroad. It was a system of people who helped **slaves** escape. People in the Underground Railroad provided food, clothing, transportation, and safe places for **fugitive**, or runaway, slaves to stay.

No one really knows how the Underground Railroad got the name. One legend credits a slave catcher who was chasing a slave in the 1830s. When the slave quickly slipped out of sight, the catcher said the slave must have traveled on a secret railroad under the ground.

Underground also means secret. People secretly worked in the Underground Railroad.

In the mid-1800s railroads were becoming popular ways to travel in the United States. So people used railroad terms to identify parts of the Underground Railroad system.

Homes and churches were **stations** on the Underground Railroad where fugitive slaves could hide and rest.

The Milton House Inn, built by Joseph Goodrich, was used to hide and transport runaway slaves due to its close proximity to a well traveled transportation line.

Fugitive slaves were called **passengers**. Those who helped the slaves were called **agents**, and those who guided them were **conductors**. **Station keepers** were people who provided places for the slaves to stay as they traveled North to seek freedom.

Freedom Fact!

The Underground Railroad was not run by a single person or group. The system was made up of many people, secret routes, meeting places, and safe houses.

Chapter 2

SLAVERY

The first slaves arrived in America in 1619 by boat. Men and women were captured in Africa, forced to leave their homes, and brought to America. As this young country grew so did the number of slaves.

UNITED STATES SLAVE TRADE.

Slaves were the legal property of their owners, called **masters**. They were often whipped for little or no reason. Some were beaten to death.

Slaves lived under strict laws. They could not own property. Most were not allowed to learn to read and write, and children of slaves became slaves.

Slaves could be bought and sold. The slave families were often separated when a parent or child was sold and moved to another **plantation**, a large farm. When slaves were sold, they often never saw their families again.

The master's family lived in a large house. Slave families usually had tiny shacks with a dirt floor to call home.

Slaves worked from sunup to sundown for no pay. They survived on little food and their clothing was often ragged. They had no control over their lives. Their owners decided where they lived, the work they did, and how they lived.

Plantation Life

Most slaves could not leave the plantation without a pass given by their master. Many were not allowed to gather in groups of more than five. They could not testify in court against their owners. Slaves had little hope for freedom because they were enslaved for life.

The states in the North and South had many differences.

Northern states had an economy based on industry and business so more people lived in cities. People worked in steel mills and for the railroads. They also manufactured goods, such as steam engines, guns, and flour.

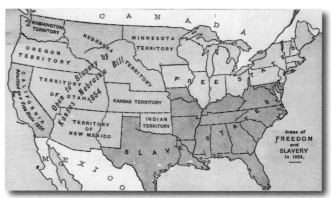

The United States 1854.
■ *Free States*
■ *Slave States*
■ *Open to Slavery*

In the South, more people lived in rural areas. The main industry was farming. Most of the slaves lived in southern states where they worked as farmhands.

Another big difference was the idea of slavery. Many people living in the North wanted slavery abolished, or stopped. The South depended on slaves to run the farms, so many people in the South wanted slavery to continue.

Freedom Fact!

Slaves in the North could learn to read and write. They usually were trained in a skill, such as carpentry, blacksmithing, or cooking, but some were often whipped and sold by their masters. Vermont was the first state to abolish slavery. State by state, the North freed the slaves living there. By the late1700s, all slaves living in the northern states were free.

The United States was divided on the slavery issue. The northern states were called **free states** because the African-Americans living in the North were free. The southern states were was called **slave states** because almost all the African-Americans were slaves.

The invention of the cotton gin in 1793 led to the growth of slavery in the South. The machine removed seeds from cotton. This made cotton more profitable so more cotton was grown. Plantation owners began working a larger number of slaves, and the slave trade increased.

In 1790 the U.S. census reported 697,897 slaves. In 1810 there were 1.2 million slaves. The number increased by 70 percent in twenty years. This increase correlates to the invention of the cotton gin.

An engraving from Harper's Magazine *in 1869 titled "The First Cotton Gin."*

Abolitionists were a group of people who wanted slavery to end immediately. Most abolitionists lived in the North. They believed slavery was wrong. Abolitionists made speeches and wrote articles and books about the cruelty of slavery. People became more aware of the conditions of slavery in the South.

But slaves in the South didn't hear the speeches. They couldn't read the articles and books. Instead, they heard stories about abolitionists that were passed along.

William Lloyd Garrison

William Lloyd Garrison was the founder of the Anti-Slavery Society. He also published an abolitionist newspaper in Massachusetts called *The Liberator*.

William Lloyd Garrison
(1805–1879)

Issue No.1, The Liberator, *1831*

In the 1830s, many people worked in the Underground Railroad, including free blacks, fugitive slaves, abolition groups, and whites who wanted to help the slaves.

Rumors and stories continued to spread to the slaves in the South. They heard that people were ready to help them travel north to a free state, where slavery was abolished. That meant traveling by foot across slave states where slavery was legal.

Josiah Henson (1789–1883)

Freedom Fact!

Josiah Henson, a runaway slave, described his journey this way, "I would start out of my sleep in terror, my heart beating against my ribs, expecting to find the dogs and slave-hunters after me." Josiah found his freedom in Canada. Once there, Josiah became involved in the Underground Railroad helping more than 200 other slaves find freedom.

Chapter 3

ESCAPE TO FREEDOM

By the 1840s more slaves were risking their lives to escape. The call to freedom was worth the risk for thousands of slaves.

Slaves watched for the best opportunity to escape so they could travel a few miles without being missed.

Owners offered large rewards for fugitive slaves. Most were caught and returned.

They had no maps to follow and no guides. Sometimes they got lost and traveled for two weeks to find a place that they could have walked to in a couple of days.

George Washington

The first record of the Underground Railroad was written by General George Washington in 1786. This was before he became the first president of the United States. One of his slaves escaped from Mount Vernon, his home in Virginia. He wrote, "a society of Quakers in the city, formed for such purposes, have attempted to liberate a slave who escaped."

George Washington
1732–1799

Some slaves escaped after they got passes to visit family members on other plantations.

Some chose the week of Christmas to escape, because they got time off from work and could travel a day or more without being missed. But traveling north in winter without suitable clothing and transportation was dangerous.

Slaves escaping to the North through southern swamps during U.S. Civil War.

Slaves often escaped on Saturday night in warm months. Many did not have to work on Sunday morning so they had more hours to travel before their masters realized they were gone.

Since slaves did not know the territory they were traveling, they had to rely on their wits.

Abolitionists were vital to the survival of fugitive slaves and their attempts at freedom. This image by artist Charles T Webber (1825–1911) depicts abolitionists Levi Coffin, his wife Catherine White, and Hannah Haydock leading a group to freedom.

Escaping in the black of night was the safest because darkness protected them. If the sky was clear, the slaves followed the North Star. On cloudy nights, they felt for moss on the trunks of trees because moss grows on the north side.

They traveled with just the clothes on their backs. Some wore several layers. Briar thickets and biting dogs tore clothes to rags quickly. Berries and other foods that grow wild provided some food.

This image known as the Stampede of Slaves from Hampton to Fortress Monroe *is from 1861 during the Civil War. It depicts slaves carrying all their possessions and running toward a river bank in the dead of night hoping to cross a bridge that led to freedom.*

Masters used bloodhounds, dogs with a keen sense of smell, to chase fugitive slaves. But the slaves used tricks to escape the dogs.

Some rubbed an onion or spruce pine on the soles of their shoes to confuse the bloodhounds. Others waded in the water so dogs could not follow their scents.

Fugitive slaves also watched for signs of those who worked the Underground Railroad. A burning lantern on a fence post or a bright quilt hanging on a fence let slaves know the house or business was a station.

Traveling between stations was difficult. Slaves often traveled 10 miles (16 kilometers) or more on foot from one station to another.

Most of the fugitive slaves who made a successful escape came from states that bordered the free states in the North. In such slave states as Kentucky, Virginia, and Maryland, the slaves had a shorter distance to travel.

A slave in Kentucky could travel to the Ohio River and cross it into Ohio, a free state. The Ohio River had many crossing points, but swimming across the river at night was dangerous.

Freedom Fact!

According to legend, the African-American song, Follow the Drinking Gourd, was used by the Underground Railroad as a code to tell the slave to follow the North Star. Gourds were used as dippers. The Big Dipper is a star formation which points to the North Star.

Excerpt from song.
"When the sun goes back
and the first quail calls
Follow the drinking gourd
The old man is a-waitin' for
to carry you to freedom
Follow the drinking gourd
When the sun goes back
and the first quail calls
Follow the drinking gourd
The old man is a-waitin' for
to carry you to freedom
Follow the drinking gourd..."

Chapter 4

HELP FOR SLAVES

Escaping to the North was much harder for slaves who lived farther south in Mississippi, Georgia, and Alabama. The distance to travel was much farther. Many of those slaves escaped to Florida where the **Seminoles**, a Native American tribe, hid them in the Everglades wetland. Some traveled further to Mexico to find freedom.

Everglades

When fugitive slaves arrived at a station, they were tired, hungry, and needed sleep. Many were confused. Some were injured or sick. Others were chased by those who were trying to capture them.

Aid to the slaves came in many forms. Some agents had false bottoms in their wagons in which slaves hid. The farmers piled hay or other items in the wagons as they transported slaves to another station.

This picture displays a wagon with a false bottom in which a fugitive slave would have traveled safely hidden under a farmer's load.

Homes and churches were used as stations. Secret closets and staircases were built so slaves could hide when slave catchers hunted for them. A woodpile may have a hiding space in its center. Some funeral processions marched along with a fugitive slave in the casket.

Freedom Fact!

Agents and slaves worked together as they planned how to travel to the next station on the route north. They developed codes to use. Certain knocks "tap-tap-tap" and passwords let the station keepers know that the person was a fugitive slave. The password "A friend with friends" was popular.

Many riverboats were piloted by free blacks, those who were not slaves. They allowed the fugitive slaves to ride without tickets and hid them so they couldn't be found.

Some used boxes and the mail service. In 1848 Henry "Box" Brown was mailed to Philadelphia. He stayed in a small, wooden crate with the top nailed shut. People knew the box was arriving so they opened it as soon as it arrived, and Henry became a free man.

Henry Box Brown

This image known as the *Resurrection of Henry Box Brown* depicts Henry's arrival in Philadelphia, Pennsylvania after being shipped from Richmond, Virginia. His journey to freedom took him approximately 26 hours.

The size of the box was 3 feet long (1 meter) by 2.5 feet deep (.7 meters) by 2 feet wide (.6 meters). That's not a lot of space!

Most of those who worked in the Underground Railroad were ordinary people, such as farmers, ministers, store clerks, and housewives.

These people did more than hide the slaves or lead them north. Some made clothes for them, collected money to buy train or boat tickets, and provided medicine and medical treatment.

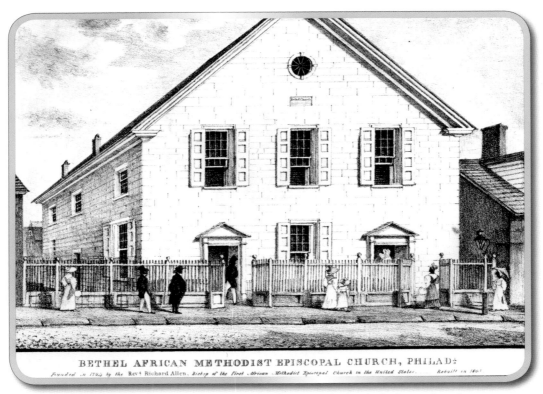

BETHEL AFRICAN METHODIST EPISCOPAL CHURCH, PHILAD?
Founded in 1794 by the Rev? Richard Allen, Bishop of the first African Methodist Episcopal Church in the United States.   Rebuilt in 1805

The Mother Bethel A.M.E. church, in Philadelphia, had a basement that was used as a stop on the Underground Railroad.

In 1850 the Fugitive Slave Law was passed. The law required fugitive slaves to be returned to their owners. The law also made it illegal to help the slaves.

Life became more difficult for those who worked on the Underground Railroad. Many were beaten or arrested and served time in jail. Banks refused to loan them money for their businesses.

Freedmen were sometimes mistaken as slaves and were beaten and killed by white slave catchers.

Slave catchers were sent to the free states in the north to hunt slaves and return them to their owners. The northern states were no longer a safe place for the slaves to live.

The Underground Railroad began helping slaves travel to **Canada**, the country that borders the U.S. to the north. In Canada, they found freedom to live, work, and own land.

Most runaway slaves were young men under the age of 35. They often fled alone or with small groups to find freedom in Canada.

Chapter 5

HEROES

Many people risked their lives helping free the slaves. The best known is Harriet Tubman, who was born a slave in Maryland. When she was twenty-nine years old, she escaped to the free state of Pennsylvania. The next year, she returned to Maryland to help her sister's family escape. She returned again to get her brothers and her parents. Tubman returned nineteen times to help over 300 slaves find freedom.

Harriet Tubman
(Birth unknown – 1913)

Harriet Beecher Stowe's book, *Uncle Tom's Cabin*, was published in 1852. In the story, a slave named Uncle Tom was sold and another slave, Eliza, escaped with her baby. The popular novel made people more aware of the Underground Railroad and the cruelty of slavery.

Uncle Tom's Cabin

Frederick Douglass was a slave who could read and write. In his book, *Life and Times of Frederick Douglass*, he told about using false papers that said he was a free man to escape. Later, he became the publisher of an abolitionist newspaper, *The North Star*.

Frederick Douglass
(1818–1895)

Quakers, a religious group, spoke out against slavery and many worked in the Underground Railroad. One Quaker, Thomas Garrett, helped about 2,700 slaves to escape.

Another Quaker, Levi Coffin, worked for thirty-three years hiding fugitive slaves in his homes in Indiana and Ohio. More than three thousand slaves hid in his homes.

Freedom Fact!

Slave owners wanted Tubman captured. They posted signs offering a $40,000 reward for her capture. In today's economy, that would be worth over 1.5 million dollars.

Levi Coffin
(1798–1877)

Chapter 6

FREE AT LAST

In 1860 Abraham Lincoln became President of the United States. More slaves were escaping, but more were captured and returned to their owners.

Abraham Lincoln (1809–1865)

The North wanted slavery abolished. The South wanted to keep slavery. So the southern states **seceded**, or separated, from the United States. The southern states formed their own government, called the **Confederacy**. The North and South fought in battles known as the Civil War from 1861-1865.

By 1860 the number of slaves had grown to 4 million. The white population was near 8 million.

People worked in the Underground Railroad at full steam during the Civil War. They continued to guide slaves to Canada and hid them from slave catchers.

The last known slave to be caught and returned to her owner was Sara Lucy Bagby Johnson. She escaped from Virginia and traveled to Cleveland, Ohio, where she was captured. Abolitionists tried to buy her freedom. Instead, she was taken back to her owner. In 1863 the northern army attacked the area and she was freed.

Sara Lucy Bagby Johnson
(circa 1833–1906)

United States Colored Troops

President Lincoln established the United States Colored Troops made up of about 200,000 African-Americans who served in the northern Army and Navy during the Civil War. Half were fugitive slaves.

Company E, 4th U.S. Colored Infantry

In 1863 President Lincoln issued the **Emancipation Proclamation**, a law that freed many slaves. In 1865 the North defeated the South and the Civil War ended. That same year, the **Thirteenth Amendment** to the Constitution abolished slavery, and the Underground Railroad was no longer needed.

As one slave explained, "The end of the war, it come just like that. You snap your fingers. How did we know it? Hallelujah broke out! Folks was singing and shouting all over."

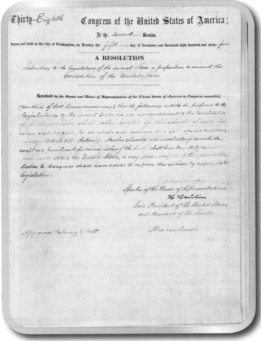

The Thirteenth Amendment to the U.S. Constitution.

Freedom Fact!

Today, we don't know the number of slaves who benefitted from the Underground Railroad, because much of the work was done in secret. Estimates place the number at 30,000-100,000. But it is known that many people risked their own lives to make the lives of thousands of slaves better.

People from all walks of life came together to form the Underground Railroad. Their work helped thousands of slaves seek freedom. Together, they made a strong force that changed lives, changed laws, and changed history.

TIMELINE

1619 —— *The first African slaves arrive in America by boat.*

1775 —— *Quakers form a society to abolish slavery.*

1786 —— *George Washington's letter is the first record of the Underground Railroad activity.*

1793 —— *Eli Whitney invented the cotton gin.*

1847 —— *The first issue of* The North Star, *an abolitionist newspaper, is published by Frederick Douglass.*

1848 —— *Henry "Box" Brown escapes from slavery. He becomes famous for the way he escaped.*

1849 —— *Harriet Tubman escapes slavery.*

1850 —— *Fugitive Slave Law is passed.*

1852 —— *Harriet Beecher Stowe's book,* Uncle Tom's Cabin, *is published.*

1860 —— *Abraham Lincoln is elected President of the United States.*

1861 —— *The first battle of the Civil War is fought at Fort Sumter, South Carolina.*

1863 —— *President Lincoln issues the Emancipation Proclamation, which freed the slaves.*

1865 —— *American Civil War ends. The 13th Amendment, which abolished slavery, is added to the U.S. Constitution.*

1881 —— *Frederick Douglass's book,* Life and Times of Frederick Douglass, *is published.*

GLOSSARY

abolitionists (ab-uh-LISH-uh-nistz): people who wanted slavery stopped immediately

agents (AY-juhntz): people in the Underground Railroad who helped slaves

Canada (CAN-uh-duh): country on the northern border of the U.S.

conductors (Kuhn-DUHK-turz): people who guided slaves on the Underground Railroad

Confederacy (kuhn-FED-ur-uh-see): a group of 11 states that declared independence from the United States just before the Civil War

Emancipation Proclamation (ii-MAN-suh-pay-shuhn prah-kluh-MAY-shuhn): a law that freed slaves

free states (FREE STATEZ): northern states in which slavery was abolished

fugitive (FYOO-ji-tiv): someone who is running away

masters (MAS-turz): slave owners

passengers (PAS-uhn-jurz): fugitive slaves on the Underground Railroad

plantation (plan-TAY-shuhn): large farm

seceded (si-SEED-ed): broke away from

Seminoles (SEM-uh-nolez): Native Americans living in Florida

slave states (SLAYV STATEZ): southern states in which slavery was legal

slaves (SLAY-vuhz): people who are the property of another

stations (STAY-shuhnz): safe places for fugitive slaves to stay as they traveled north

station keepers (STAY-shuhn KEE-purz): people in the Underground Railroad who provided safe places for fugitive slaves to stay as they traveled north

Thirteenth Amendment (THUR-teenth uh-MEND-muhnt): ratified in 1865, this amendment to the U.S. Constitution abolished slavery

Underground Railroad (UHN-dur-GROUND RAYL-rohd): a system to help slaves escape to freedom

INDEX

SHOW WHAT YOU KNOW

1. What is slavery?
2. How did the Underground Railroad help fugitive slaves?
3. Why did slaves risk their lives to escape their owners?
4. What are some ways slaves used to find their way north without maps?
5. Why did abolitionists risk their lives helping slaves?

WEBSITES TO VISIT

education.nationalgeographic.com/education/underground-railroad-interactive/?ar_a=1#

www.pbs.org/wgbh/americanexperience/features/general-article/lincolns-underground-railroad/

www.socialstudiesforkids.com/articles/ushistory/undergroundrailroad1.htm

ABOUT THE AUTHOR

Nancy Kelly Allen lives in Kentucky where she celebrates American history by writing books. For her, research is like a treasure hunt. She snoops around and digs up interesting information about people, places, and things that shaped our country's past.

Meet The Author!
www.meetREMauthors.com

www.rourkeeducationalmedia.com

PHOTO CREDITS: Title Page © LouLouPhotos; Title Page, page 4, 5, 6, 7, 9, 10, 11, 12, 13, 15, 20, 22, 24, 25, 26, 27 © Library of Congress; page 8 © history.com; page 10 © National Portrait Gallery; page 13, 16 © North Wing Pictures Archive; page 14 © bridgemanart.com; page 18 © Jeremiah Greenleaf; page 19 © Levi Coffin House and Waynet; page 21 © Mother Bethel A.M.E. Church, Richard Allen Archives, Philadelphia, PA.; page 25 © National Archives Gift Collection, George K Warken; page 27 © The Western Reserve Historical Society, Cleveland, Ohio; page 29 © National Archives

Edited by: Luana Mitten

Cover design by: Renee Brady
Interior design by: Renee Brady

Library of Congress PCN Data

The Underground Railroad / Nancy Kelly Allen
(Symbols of Freedom)
ISBN 978-1-63430-043-8 (hard cover)
ISBN 978-1-63430-073-5 (soft cover)
ISBN 978-1-63430-102-2 (e-Book)
Library of Congress Control Number: 2014953359

Printed in the United States of America, North Mankato, Minnesota

Also Available as:

ROURKE'S
e-Books